A RICKLE OF BONES

A RICKLE OF BONES

RUTH O'CALLAGHAN

Shoestring Press

Printed by imprintdigital
Upton Pyne, Exeter
www.digital.imprint.co.uk

Typesetting and cover design by narrator
www.narrator.me.uk
info@narrator.me.uk
033 022 300 39

Published by Shoestring Press
19 Devonshire Avenue, Beeston, Nottingham, NG9 1BS
(0115) 925 1827
www.shoestringpress.co.uk

First published 2020
© Copyright: Ruth O'Callaghan
© Cover image: Christine Johnson

The moral right of the author has been asserted.

ISBN 978-1-912524-65-5

ACKNOWLEDGEMENTS

My special thanks to John Lucas, author-publisher extraordinaire, for his continued advice and enthusiasm.

For Christine

Without whose love and encouragement
this book would never have happened

CONTENTS

TRANSITION

ARCHIVE

In the universe, there are things that are known, and things that are unknown,
and between them, there are doors.

William Blake.

LIMINAL

1.

Where the edges are we cannot be certain
but all possibilities exist

        though we know they are
not where light studs the walls

spikes the thistle, leaves sharp against
uneven plaster.

        We know they are
not where spindles of willow

fringe the shore while an oarsman's stroke
chronicles days

obscures margins: the river running fast.
Obscures

where other waters gather in another place
on the far side

too far for the eye to discern but we suspect
a presence

        leaves quivering
without wind, cuckoos refusing to greet spring

        though everything has its season:
daffodils give way to slash of tulips

bloodspills in discrete suburbs cleansed by rain
        where Easter camellias blaze
           red: sanguine.

2.

Let us loot logic, ransack that sly surge of doubt
inherent where knowledge defines parameters,
denies salt that seasons learning. Let us savour
the edge. Horizons are no longer without limit.
Groping beyond an encroachment of dark, faith
falters. That which is hidden is sought, not given.

Then let us sit and talk, not of things known
but of that which lies between: the threshold
where no sun stains the dusk-damson-dark,
where the willow weeps over naive days,
where the handle of the closed door remains
unturned: that which is sought is hidden.

We who have known the isolation of day, the retch
of night, must embrace that which is other, forswear
the familiar, reach into the divide. Such little courage
is needed yet we, forever, creep back toward light.
Let us choose dark's warmth where once we were
hidden: grasp what is given – although not sought.

PALINGENESIS

Spring has come
and with it a shallow hope

each shadow of resurrection
creased

in knees of old women
as they lower bones, search

for genesis unfound in a world
where forgotten

Golgotha conceals
divisions the way a cell cleaves

against itself, creates new
malignancies.

                      ***

So a neighbour will bake bread
offer to one and not another
who will leave the house

silently, intent as Judas,
diminished in his own eyes
his hurt exacting execution: action

undertaken ripples beyond the immediate
a butterfly wing causing chaos
in another country

where old women resolve
their allotted ration
                   alpha-omega:
the measure of days proportional.

RESUMPTION

The goods on display are available in-house
by catalogue and on-line: distribution international.

They will clothe you, feed you, shoe you, give you
knowledge that enables you to walk streets which you,

all-powerful, will pave with gold but those who walk
in nakedness know there is other which is not found

in a country or town or room in a town or the desert
once travelled where no road is marked. The dark

lends perception where you may stand under any star
unhoused, without direction, free from any structure

which may constrict, which may deny grasp and heft
of that, not buried within, but, as yet, unharvested.

So it was in 1887 when a child, set on a train at four years, at 5 a.m.
Hampshire to Newport, left behind a flat-stomached mother, widowed,
and one sister, elder, for whom she saved the lemon slice crowning

her sugar-bun, slapping it on the driver's window. Left at the orphanage
without family news for seven years her first returning words disturbed:
Where are the twins?

Hence a man when in unfamiliar fields or riding rivers
whose name he is unable to enunciate, feels growth

feels a current pouring through his bloodstream, hears
the echo of other steps, is certain he will leave all

he has known or has wanted, will leave all those
he has loved but not wanted, to gather the fruits of field

fish from water, will shed no tears for what he has surrendered
aware that shoots re-appear in unexpected places.

And so it is:

I have returned.

TESTIMONY

I waited for you where the silverfish swarm
in an empty house

Watching tarmac give way to dust, greyed
car fade, distant

Your thumb a ticket to unknown lands where
unknown hands wandered

Borders crossed to lie in overheated rooms
facing a cul-de-sac.

***

In fields, when stone potatoes failed, waiting
gave way to anguish

Ancestral voices, hunger-bellied, surged over
those same seas

No salt to savour strangers denied tenements
waiting demolition.

***

I waited with my thirst and in my hunger I waited
living another's story

I sought comfort applying nettles to wounds
caustic words

To love, which had no meaning for one who stayed
worked, changed

8

Beds, made sure soft feathers became hard, cold
the mattress thin.

***

I have held time where flatlands remained unbroken
and horizons crept behind

Unopened windows, hidden by trees whose leaves
losing colour

drift over the dry well where waiting old women greet
me as one.

SURMISE

Yes, there was a slow dance – under a glitter ball –
the Unobtainable One nestled into a shoulder
who searched over for some other unobtainable one
whose laugh shimmered, teeth perfect white.

It was spring waiting for summer: the light burning the earth
the earth swallowing the light: shriven.
                                    After, in the reed beds
we heard the secretive bittern or his visiting distant cousin
the throat full with song, each booming note strung out, striking

dusk as car lights over an undressed window caress a ceiling.
That year, summer never came: the song diminished, ceased.
Sometimes a wind stirs the trees, brings remembrance
of an unknown descant unspooling on the air:

in the passing quiet of an autumn evening a sudden
recognition of something other, of that *perhaps*,
of what we are now:
                        I am unable to recall our word
                                        for *remember*.

                        ***

Now there is only an old woman in an old house
– has this been said before? A poet reads so much
all is melded in the mist, one inhabits
                            the other's space

the body released, resurrected, the poetry passed on
transubstantiated in another's mind.
                              (Can even Eliot lay sole claim
                    In the end is my beginning
when in the beginning was the Word: the clay and pith of all?)

Or here, in this clear cutting, with this poet
                                        whom I have to stop
reading before he takes me
                    to a place I can no longer visit.

GIVEN THE NARRATIVE

                    the fish farm out in the fjord
lights set at a distance from each other
one a cluster the other slight, single

                                    balanced
on the landing stage, both flashing in unison
each catching the eye of the night watcher
– perhaps a poet unable to sleep, desperate

for warmth or words that will carry him
                                    into a dream
world where the one woman he has ever loved
neither his present wife nor past wives, nor her

to whom he was betrothed but never married
nor the one before that whom he impregnated
in woods
      without smell of pine or sound of birdsong

but mounted
on dank leaves,
                    devoid of even the jacket
he carefully draped on an overhanging branch after

equally carefully
                    placing on the ground the fish caught
in a lake of commensurate depth to this fjord,
                                    before

pushing her beside, jaws agape, predatory
murmuring perfidious promises, leaving her
an unmarried, never-to-be-married, mother: no, not her
                                    but the one

before
the one who kept her private places from him
        allowing contact only in public spaces: the one
whose threshold he'd never been invited to cross

despite her passionate nature
her concern over Albert Herring, Mrs Pike and others
                    of the ilk
whom Britten sent to sea, whose shanties

called to her
        when he finally inveigled her to dinner
the one who, as he was uncorking
            Pouilly Fume

musing
upon the catch of the day
        predicting the aftermath of dessert
he hears the snick of the latch

                hurries from the kitchen
to find a craze of blue on her plate, the black fish skin
              draped
neatly over one side –

that is the one
        he seeks in the fjord beyond the fish farm
this watcher in the night whose narrative
        begins with lights set apart from each other….

FUGUE

He stood where snow banked damp walls
waited till slush pooled beneath wheels
on an abandoned barrow, watched slow

rot of wood leak brown, the sledge rust
the ground, untrodden, incarnadine
bright and bitter as the thirst of winter.

***

In this sparse Norwegian town a thread of gossip
withdraws certainty, each second fuel to the idle
ambiguity of tongues. Barren silence transforms:

the alchemy of rumour becomes the salt of truth
the insubstantial, immutable. Disclosed, a secret
retold slants, gives rise to self-fulfilling prophecy.

***

In the shadowless yard a shovel lay broken
the handle severed, the blade bent, too blunt
to attack compacted ice: treacherous, black

transparent, the way a mourner's coat shrouds
signs of grief within or clouds cover the fjord
where her limbs had once cleaved winter water.

ARCHIVE

Perhaps we do not remember the loss
but in evening still or the bone silence
of an eyeless exhibit – depths dragged,
habitat invaded, displayed in museum -
there will be a tug in a part of you
and you will be thrust back to surface,
a lost tourist wandering a shuttered city
where the petit point of eyes intersect:
each step toward the distant harbour
marked: an intimation of mist intimidates.
Only a frail bridge allows hope: hovering.

Older men declare war. But it is youth that must fight and die.

Herbert Hoover

ANTHEM

We need no preface. The prologue
was already written before we were born.
You can see by our now-dull eyes how we were
moulded to shoulder responsibility, to accede
to each fight/flight theory they accorded to whim.
                                        We sallied forth:
Ta-Rooh! Ta-Rooh! We are those who burbled
spittle as hymns graced our baby blue bonnets:
Faith of Our Fathers laced with *Humpty Dumpty*
replaced by bonhomie, regimental songs, replaced
again, again, again, again by *Abide With Me*:
helmets swiftly reinstated after the hasty burial.

So many hasty burials: hasty rituals in so many lands
friend Death had difficulty deciding destination – first
a clandestine visit, say… mingling in malarial jungle?
Or aerial bombardment? Carpet saturation, no pardon?

Yet in death we *lived*! In the very moment we died
we knew the quickening of life, the catch in the crotch
that he who survived later felt in fields,
face facing earth, underneath him all that he desired.
                            On top. Over the top.
Death or love, love or death, all feeds the earth,
whether above or shovelled beneath.
                            All we want is to go back,
to know we can return not in surrender but in belief:
irrational: irredeemable. Take from us our dull eyes.

***

Denied, we can only witness the quiet dying of love
where once it bled in different fields: indifferent, untended:
the weight of all that flesh, the weight of all that mind.

17

Retreating, we fled to the beach where now we play,
shells sharp beneath the careful towel that cannot smother
the merciless whine once heard over other skies, bright,
treacherous. We cannot escape strafing memory:
the beach laden with bodies, sand-stuffed mouths agape.
We pull pellets of white from the body of bread: stuff mouths,
drink wine. How can we eat in the glare of their blind eyes?

Who will judge us in our nakedness. In our nakedness
we cry *Brother! Brother! Are we not all from the same*
Mother who bore the same pain? Does not the same
Sun regard us all as we palm the bread, drink the wine?

***

Remember Smythe? He who swifted through barefoot days
and fields of wheat, now pauses in a patch of sunlight
on kitchen parquet, the back step too steep to contemplate.
His halting feet cannot traverse the untrodden lawn,
                              cannot embrace the rat
caught in pyracantha and chicken wire sleeving the wall
– its cry slices the air, releases mandatory memory. He defies
the marauding mob whose howls seize his ears.
He prizes thorns. Such was worn by One despised,
One who bequeathed droplets of red to stain the earth
between two thieves: thieves will not deceive *him*,
he will hold the line, deny access, trumpet his bequest:
he will leave the redness of berries. *Ta-Rah! Ta-Rooh!*

***

And what of us who are left? We who now cower in the shelter
of peace to spend lives in fear of being caught unawares
in the backyard privvy listening to neighbours call
through pre-fab walls, hear feet slacken on stairs
by our door, as we slip into a dim room farthest
from plaster flaking when the lodger above
practises midnight-dance steps.

Deprived
of privacy we turn up the volume on the Home programme,
select a symphony on the Third to forget brave (such irony!)
words heard within the absurd tin-jangle on Whitehall-wallahs
beribboned chests – touchstone of victorious endeavour –
that was our antiphony, is our requiem. Touchstone. Tombstone.

We who are neither living nor dying submit
to seasonal rituals, unreasonable demands
on those whose time was denied despite
survival in dry fields where now vines feed,
flourish where death of love left love of death.
For those who remain the smell of fresh-baked bread,
promise of ripe cheese, savours us to the kitchen, surly
from labour, to drink rough red under this sun, blinded
by the glare from dead eyes rising from this very soil.
Eyes of the first to fall, who, by our side, cried
                    Attack! Attack!
So we fall to. Devour all laid on the checkered cloth
courtesy of shelter given to us survivors by the lee
of *their* assault. They were not left to shumble along,
blinkered, the way Smythe's horse stumbles toward
the knacker's yard, while we evaluate the hereafter
where motion ceases in that place of ceaseless motion:
in their remembrance we eat this bread, drink this wine.

                         ***

Snow-crooked, the tree curves into the wind: wind-bent too,
we climb the road to the cemetery gates, the incline steep,
petrol station carnations droop despite chill of summer heat.

                         ***

While we pursued small pieces of silver to dispel
our darkness, they gambolled in Elysian fields.
We, who do not deserve even Tartarus, slaver
in shadow but, at our behest they shall rise not
to question how we live but to bequeath us life

19

for all deaths bequeathed: we who remain lost
in prayer, pray not to lighten our darkness
                              but to darken our lightness

as we wait for the promised release
of eternal peace in this stubborn summer
pray for a perpetual Spring
where we may move in perpetuity
where manifold poppies unfold

where untold reminiscences remain
in dark rooms in shady pubs
where old men nurse warm halves
where the bitter barmaid keens
for a lover who lay with her in a field
his flying jacket under her head
she purses purple lips to admit a kiss
sees sunken mouths in shrunken bodies.
Not these. Not these, dear God, not these.

***

Folded like dead roses their mouths feed on soft parts.

***

A possibility of… steak? rare or even blue?
on which our speculation dwells, leads to
that which age necessitates; abdication.
Fleet time devours timid days yet still
such abject hesitancy holds fast,
increases with each passing
year while feet slow over
autumn leaves that bend
head and will: how soon
the wind of change
dwindles to
a winding
sheet.

OFFENSIVE

They have all fallen now:
leaves wet-bright in spring submit
to summer's burn, the sap of autumn:

at the wind's shift they were left
for the gardener's rake to rattle drily
into order: compost: no names attached.

LOSS

We cannot come again to our woods
where the lark and white birch hold
true rapture. Though a waste of years
will quicken, death will not hurry but will
rupture time, not to salve, to forget
those selves we were, but to bleed these
of any love retained: the vein collapsed.

YOUTH

The days are passing by, running by,
we are paralysed by heat, by power,
by innocence, by our own unforgiving

flower which allows no respite, shows
no mercy to lives once bright but now,
craving lost youth, cripples: our bitter
sun declines, even our shadow fades.

INTERCHANGE

Ah's sorry ah kick yo stick, man. Shit,
ah di'n't meanta send yo into no orbit
ah was flyin' wid me po'try. 'S wickid.
Wanna give yo ear? Hear me wor'z?

And now a surly street youth spews *wor'z?*
to some *kinda beat?* Poetry? What a cheek!
All those deaths freely bequeathed… For what?

Yo know wad, bro, yo's 'xactly as you seem.
Yo never heard o' the Man an' his Dream?
Let me tell you 'bout the man an' his Dream….

Martin Luther King? I know *'xactly* whom you mean,
a keen reformer. I'm not one to judge by your skin.
In that last *circus* Ghurkas never shirked their duty,
fought like a white…. All regular soldiers. No others.

Dat's 'xactly wat he means. We one brother
'neath de skin. Why yo' look only de colour?
Yo need courage to look beyond see black's
white while white's on'y light'r shade o' black.

Ridiculous! I don't like your attitude, young man.
An' yo don' give me no latitude, O-l-d sold-jer.
Yo say yo fight for freedom 'n dat is de dream
But when it come it to wad it mean….?

It means that you are free to speak as you please.
It means that you are free to make a choice.
It means that we fought for this *voice* you flaunt…
but at what cost. You'll never know how many lives I ost….

I sho' don' wanna inta'fere wid what yo sayin'
but bro' I can hear yo pain praying to be free
same wid me an' me bros when we rhyme

wid dat ting we talkin' 'bout what we feel.
No big deal but yo betta lis'en wad we say.
… 'Kay we ain't no Shakes-speare …

I'm amazed you even know his name let alone claim….

Bro, ol' Bill talk wid me frequently, we's kinda…in-
ti-mate. Day don' go by when I don' sigh over wad
de ol' Bill say. He occupy mah time. He occupy mah min'.
His wor'z? Wicked, de way you sez, not wickid like I state…

How dare you compare your jingle to what he creates!
Your meaningless rhyme won't stand the test of time!

Bro' y'know' yo jus' show yo got de rhythm, now, chill.

How dare the likes of you tell *me* what to do. Standing
there in that insolent pose, who do you think you are?

Mah name is Thomas Stearns. Why yo look like that?
Yo learn som'tin' everyday. Sold-jer. Dis pose? Dis stance?
I chose it fo' mah po'try. Ah has an inheritance. Mah name.

Are you trying to claim affinity with Eliot, a classic poet?
How can you, a mere pubescent boy, match your lame words
with the divinity in *Ash Wednesday* or his graphic journey
to witness the Nativity. Thomas Stearns you are nescient!

Not so, bro. Ah's sentient. To de extent o' prescience.
You notice…sorry bro, no-tiss f' you wan' me to keep
mah stance, yo man go off on a riff, seduced by sound
sho'ly as de Hound o' Heaven *pursued de udda one.*

Udda? I shudda! If you are cognisant with such matters
Why do you persist in such idle street corner chatter?

Dere yo go 'gain, bro. We don' diss past conventions
dat ain't our intention. We jus' take de structure 'n B-l-a-st
it apart . That's Art, brother, Art sister. We changin' 'way

it's gonna be. No diff'rence to TSE way he jumps 'bout
in dat Wasteland *den jus gi's us a list to fill a cupla lines*
                        you want me to
                                sink
                                  to
                                that
                                  dis
                                tinc
                                tion?

No, bro, Ah do'n' suffer from no bibliophobia
ah's a logomachist. Me 'n mah boys sing
street corners hear our fears 'n our longings
in consonants 'n assonance. Our pre-sent-ation
'n innovation do 'way wid preconceptions, carry
de lang-widg inta tomorrow. Yo better follow
'cos we strippin' de facade of Harvard prosody
takin' 'way de dreamin' spires 'cos lang-widg
is ever self re-invention 'n dat is our intention.

Gordon Bennet! That *is* some statement.
An all fro' standin' on dis pavement. YO!

APRIL 3 '81

Christ ain't riding' his Harley here
or burnin' down Coldharbour Lane
Brixton don' need no messiahs
we got de drugs, de feefs, de liars
we had de hunger, we had de bricks
dey had de hatred – we burnt dat bitch
                    FRONTLINE

We took de streets – swamp '81
ain't gonna stop no black born son
we had de roots, we had de fire
ev'ry man his own messiah
no passifyin' fro' politico thugs
dey de drugs, de feefes, de liars.
                    BIG TIME

IMPROVISATION WITH TWO MASKS

1. Rehearsal

Let loose upon a world where Janus
has many faces, the director whispers
and the mask inside the mask unknots

a ravelled creature within, possibilities
for pretence unfold – knowing reality
trembles when shared amongst many:

knowing a shadow shadows each mask
and each must elicit its own portion
in a corpus of deferred satisfaction

having mastered the science of silence
having remained impartial: a pulse of deletions
– an unsettled geography of geographies.

2. Preparation

Diamond rough will glow, will reflect
the art bestowed upon it: the cutter's
precision creates facets, submits it to bruiting,

cleaving, to be polished by first one then another.
Behind its final radiance lies the face
of many men – and its own face is many

according to how the seller slants the stone
towards the light, how he holds for a moment
the memory of this commodity's true state before

folding it into his fist. He tightens his grip, whispers
he needs the currency it offers, so imprisons it
– behind clear glass facing the world's window.

3. Rohingya

Let's look at it this way. Exile on an isle
on the edge of action and desire, a smooth
face mirrored in the lake's smooth water

allows no faraway thunder or fractious sea
to break a vow but undertakes to resign
family and friends for a nation, for the world's

service: BBC. Though we know a wise woman
does not carry a flaming torch in a strong wind
we also know that solitude may whisper one

sacrifice is sufficient: silence may mask many ambitions
transposition lies in a stretch of water, transforms
innocence, power: remains a silent witness.

HUMAN CHAIN

Dublin 1916: Riga 2011: Las Vegas 2017

A new commandment I give you: Love one another
– John 13: v. 34–35

Bullet holes riddled the side of our 4* superior
bringing you back, belly flat, squint eye cocked,
the barrel of your 1871 Mauser an easy match,
you declared, for those bastards' 3.1 Webleys,
your voice stuttering after Pearse's Proclamation,
the stone of GPO affording temporary protection.
                    But
                    this isn't Dublin '16
                    or even Derry '69
– apprentices marching, your grandsons stoning –
it is tourist-trap Riga: these holes hold remembrance,
denote self-determination.
                             Given grisly details
we allow justification of the nation's action, follow
the guide inside where *Eurochannel* flickers over
The Strip, pans to Mandalay Bay Hotel, 32nd floor,
                    But
                    this isn't featuring
                    Vegas highlights
or maybe it is: a solitary man reaps the Harvest:*
                         fans scatter before seeds
from his 23 souped-up semi-automatic rifles: a man
who voted for a man determined to create freedom
to possess power by guns, bombs – a man who can
flick his switch, a switch bigger than any other man's.†
                    59 dead
                    501 injured.
                    So far.

* 1st October 2017 Harvest music festival massacre in Las Vegas
† 3rd January 2018 Trump boasts his nuclear capacity greater than
that of Kim Jong-un

HOTEL

A door clicks down an unspecified
length of corridor, carpet thick
enough to smother secrets

occupants whom we will never meet
but who we imagine, clandestine
assignments undertaken

not necessarily governmental
not necessarily other....

THE ART OF WAR

Have you witnessed Herr Groningen directing the orchestra?
I have
    testified to the deadly accurate rat-a-tat-tat
Of his black baton.

Have you heard Madame Maria Theresa at La Scala?
I have
    succumbed to her sublime soprano
Demanding death.

Have you heard Anna Kanosonia as Coppelia?
I have
    watched her pointed toes pirouette gaily
In a bayonet thrust.

While on the boulevard Bordeaux-rouge visages bemused by
Ankles of beribboned-girls, raise glasses to dancers
Goose-stepping the Champs Elysée.

Have you watched Herr Groningen smile?
His baton
        quavers slightly as he surveys the debris for whom
He is conducting.

Transition

JACOB

Darkness clothed him as it did me.

 I had sought solitude,
sent all I possessed to the far side: children, concubines,
cattle not offered to Esau: my wives. A wedge of dusk fell
as I settled within a cleft of rock watching shadows, wide
as sepulchre stones, sweep the ground. A crease of wind
lifted my prayer, for pray I must being dispossessed: love
fled with possession of a birthright.

 A shadow weighed upon
my shoulder, the way a bird of prey quartering the ground
is relentless, precise. Then a scald of cold tightened skin.
I was bound to a man, leaf-thin, whom I could not grasp,
who slipped from my grip as easily as water drawn fresh
from the well quells the hunter's thirst. He forced my head
towards his but

 I knew not to look into those eyes; knew

to fear what I might find there. A traveller's instinct.

 He tripped
my legs but I would not submit. Entwined, we bit into the dust
beyond the safety of my rock. The ground was a litter of thorns,
thistles whose purple pricked his skull, pricked blood,
droplets slid down his face but still he would not stop.
He smashed into me. I felt my bone break, the pain snaking.
My hand thrashed the ground, was guided to a blade of stone:
I slashed. He twisted. The stone cracked into his side.

 A drag of grey
across the sky gave way to dawn: the air layered: still.

 I saw a thread
of muscle quiver in his throat as if he would speak. He croaked *Release*.
I considered. Refused. We had fought until each sinew, each

 limb knew
intimacy with the other's. We were brothers. I would seek a blessing
that will hold me in stead to seek forgiveness from my birth brother.

He would not give it to me, Jacob, but would bestow it on one
                                            who is called
by another name, one who has repented, persevered, fought in
                                            darkness:
one who is reckoned as a force in the eyes of the Lord, in the
                                        eyes of man.

They say I have seen the face of God, of JHWH, but to me he
                                        was younger
than our Deity, the limbs firm, strong, perhaps of one who is
                                    yet to come.
I am not a prophet but who is to say our old orthodoxies are
                                    immutable?

They say you cannot gather grapes from thorns or pluck figs
                                        from thistles
but, as a tongue of sunlight destroyed the final dark, I found in
                                        this place,
of thorns and thistles, a deletion of self. Such absorption I
                                    have untravelled.
I have found a country where clarity of light permits no
                                distance, no dominion

36

EVE

He's gone again. No explanation. No, *Would you like to come?*
I know I've been blessed. He told me so. I know I owe him
my life – I am but a rib from his side. My life is his gift.

He did mention that. Once or twice. He can be fun! If he's
                                                around. If not…
I've little choice in what to do. *He* named each creature so they all
refuse to come, choose not to play, if it's not *his* voice that calls.

And the serpent seeing the woman wander alone
let loose a coil of words from beneath the tree, each
one a whisper to allure her curiosity, to draw her close:

The whole garden is in abeyance for the absent one.
Walking amongst such endless abundance there's nothing
to be done except to go to and fro. Do you not tire of such vacuity?

I know I shouldn't complain but I have feelings I can't explain.
                                                I understand
he needs his friend, the one he says we owe, who gave our law
                                                to live by,
who gave, sorry, *bestowed*, us this land but I need something more.

And the serpent saw that the woman, alone, without garment,
without purpose, having no mate to idle an hour, followed his sound,
drifted towards the tree where all that is as yet unknown is to be found.

He says his dominion over all allows him certain rights. No
                                                doubt it does.
But what am I to do when seeds spring from the ground
                                                ready-watered,
source unknown. Even fruit falls from the trees, falls into our hands?

He says I'm a malcontent. I'm not. I just want to reinvent
those days
when play is his sole desire. To find a purpose when he retires,
when I am left, bereft. I'm restless. I don't have any say.

And the serpent, seeing her, chose one word above all other
and the woman heard the word and the word, soft on his lips,
became soft on her lips so the serpent came close and the word was…

…Knowledge!

And the serpent saw the word swell within the woman,
and the serpent saw she knew the absent other had denied her
this fruit, this beauteous fruit whose fragrance lingered upon the air.

I dared! I dared to bite. Its sweetness surprised. *He* said it
would be hard.
Bitter…. When he saw – my choice! – that I knew, *his* voice
was hard.
Bitter…. But I teased him. If I was to *please* him, he had to bite. Hard.

His eyes opened wide. Then he gave me a stare I'd never seen
before.
The day wasn't cold but I shivered. His eyes…flickered. I was
aware….
My boldness fled. The snake snickered. Furled himself on a fig leaf.

IMPENDING

Friday was the worst day. The crowds baying,
horses jittering stones down the hill, the dogs
licking each others sores until a sudden spurt

when the spear was wrenched: no cry or sound
but the soldier blenched, threw himself down,
ignored the centurion who, furious, slashed

him where he lay but still the soldier refused
to obey, to rise. They say the itinerant spoke
of a different resolve, boasted, *I will be held,*

killed by elders, but on the third day, raised.
His words lacked judgement. He who carries
a load of hay should always avoid sparks.

***

The town is quiet today. Those who had watched
now huddle in houses, their eyes wide, unwilling
to give tongue to what they had witnessed.

After, those who did it were also silent, shifted feet,
looked to their hands, amazed, then hid them under
until the one they call Borrachio hefted a skin, *oxos*

poured deep into his gullet swifter than that offered
to the one who hung there. Another stripped the skin,
licked the inside and spat, demanded *gleukos*

but the sweetest wine turned sour before it reached
his throat. The strongest drink, bought with the last
denarius, did not allow the peace they sought.

They say one, who was not present, hung himself.
We do not yet know why. He was rich. Silver scattered
beneath his feet. Perhaps he saw he was ill-advised

to follow an itinerant but if we are lonely – apparently
he had no friends – a kind word binds us fast. The town
remains dark. Tomorrow, it is said, the sun will rise....

SLOUGH

This is a time of rain, of sorrow
of knowing and not knowing

when all that is gained is lost
and the loss remains forever

elusive. Unprepared, numbed,
every memory bereft: eclipsed.

Brittle with misery we seek sun,
days where we can stride hills

barefoot, grasp thistles, disturb
skylarks in wheaten fields: suffer.

THE GARDENS

These gardens do not grow
borage, sage or rosemary but
time, expediency, expectancy.

***

So how do City slickers greet/grind this god-given day
drear as that when the sun had not yet risen but
the Footsie fallen?
　　　　　　　They keep faith, don city suits
or stilettos – it is rumoured bearded Harold has both –
scuttle for a bus but the crowd at the stop
allowed no boarding so a quick slop of coffee
in Costa's cardboard cup confirms eco-credentials –
refutes responsibility for a whale pregnant with plastic
threshing in a dying ocean…but let us not linger
on notions of extinction….

***

Aah, that we could return to the Garden
The sway of trees giving forgiveness
in letting of leaves; so we let blood
grieving for unremembered acts.

The past is not reversible. Reprieve?
Impossible. Clemency is not merciful:
reprisal lies in governance of its granting.
Lethe. Lethe. Let us bathe forever.

***

3 p.m, It is not tea they take midway to ease
the day, nor is the white, heated in the spoon,
sugar. Flame and crackle serve to ignore
other travesties that happened at that same hour

– recorded in a dusty book. Brokers, crucified
when Nikkei notes Nasdaq falls, Shanghai threatens
and that Holy of Holies the NYSE has swollen
beyond Fanny May, Freddie Mac's sustainability,
feel suicidal: then it will not only be the temple curtain
rent but the temple itself. A tsunami of bodies plunge
from high as money's calvary sweeps the world:
daily resurrection from bed has no meaning.
                         Yet not all rise to the crew of clock.

Victor shakes his greying rats tail
free of elastic band, contemplates
not the rising sun but the falling
stack of chips, lives once more
the croupier's clarion call, clings
diminishing hope on a final card,
feels the dealer's rake scrape
the baize, demolishing dreams.
He climbs into his boyhood bed,
single, box room, all others let
to lodgers… apologies… *P.G's*:
mother's terraced pre-war house
BULGES.

Not so the parsonage: a thin-lipped vicar
slips along dim passages, administers a last
last week's wafer to Mrs. Bareface, wipes
her slack-mouth-spit from his manicurist

-fashioned nails, his only indulgence, raises
eyes to Him, hanging crowned, dusty, retreats
to a low altar devoid even of a solitary server
to hand him water before his semi-closed lips
purse to approach the chalice rim, a grimace
wincing at the aroma of cheap wine: of Blood.

Not so the presbytery: red-faced Flynn
swills his dregs of brandy, contemplates
his sermon, his abject failure to answer

the child Christy observing that, scientifically,
given relative dimensions, the improbability
of a house holding many mansions; regrets
the consequent cuff to grinning Jimmy Flynn,
regrets rumours that abound with the mother,
single, dead, and that distinctive Flynn nose....
Light floods the hall as he attends the door:
he offers the beggar his one warm coat.

Slashed cloak? You're just half-measure
St. Martin-de-Tours. Stop/search? Swords
fetch a 4 year stretch, more if you're military:
bearded Harold, fresh faced in Afghanistan,
served in Syria, hid his face behind fungi,
ran amok in a dress, the child in the ruins
pursuing, pursuing, pursuing –
                         and only old Flynn,
drunken old Flynn, listens, offers sanctuary
in a presbytery stacked with communion wine,
no half measures here as Harold repeats,
                         repeats, repeats, re....

...The sun ever higher, a tea shop, replete
with chai and bowls, offered small respite
yet the hut, the overturned chair, the child
at the door's edge, the soldier's shadow
showed....
              There's no return to the Garden?

***

Flynn respects his Sunday sheep. Takes the text,
It is easier for a camel etcet. They bow their heads
– to check the Heng Seng. Volatile! Extortionate
rate for yen, trading won't wait until London opens.
A swift swipe averts disaster as Flynn exhorts poverty,
petitions for generosity, munificence: they thank God
for i-phones, for all technology that increases wealth.
To ensure continuance they place a note in the plate.

And so we never lose the child in each of us.

                                         Faith lies
in avoiding cracks in paving where weeds grow, knowing
heaven lies

not in soil but solidity – which brings us back to suits,
fragrance exuding from every one as they guide
a skip-jump child towards the prized primary.

They do not wither once attendance is no longer imperative
but move on, impervious, while those who remain observe
expensive City shoes have now removed the threat to patent

from chestnuts, shed on this suburban earth by heaven-sent
ancient trees – *Fell the buggers. They clutter gutters.*
Is *they* a soubriquet for the crones and codgers who refuse
to die, to release property in this desirable neighbourhood?
We need to buy for Oliver and Olivia, before rising prices
force migration to Barking, Brent or Barnet. We have seen

at our Cotswold retreat, how a cleaner is not to be had
for love or money. During the week the village is deserted!
And so Fiona and Philip, Malcolm and Melanie greet each day
with moneyed-trepidation, without any salutation to any rising Sun.

PAUSE

In this space we will deliberate
on the distraction of absence
how the unsaid cements

the moment, how abstraction
from each casual utterance
renders those few words

potent, lends action impotence:
do not seek solace, rather try
to catch the wind in a net.

CLOSE KNIT: TANK TOPS

1.

Shit, dad. 'Kay. Know it's *illiterate* to swear
'n you'd rather *Father*. Don't wear your ass
out trying to make me you. Fifty's past it!
Going all out for the biggie 'n what you got?
What you done? I'm not the five year old son
who so cried when you yelled. Then you held
my hand. Soft. Now you're squeezing my balls.
Testicles. Genitals. Whatever prissy way you
wanna say it. What I want is music 'n pussy.
Not necessarily in that order. There is no order.
They come, 'scuse the pun, as one. Synonymous.
See. Can do the semantics. You taught me well
but there's no way I'm following you. I do drums.
A pro. We got gigs. We're solid. We're out there.
With all those chicks. We jus' flick our hair....
Yeah. *Non, je ne regrette rien.* That French bird
knew a thing or two. Not like you. Poor old tosser.
Bet you go back when they give you that clock.
40 years! You'll miss the gos. Who's late back?
Who's swerved on fines?. Rivetin'! 40 fuckin' years.
Where else can you pick the hairs from your ears?
Come on, dad? Same old, same old? Take a trip.
Take mum. *Don't* do that *auberge.* Alpine walks.
All trees 'n mountains. Talk about bein' a goat!
Thought I was a kid. Pun! You were fun with words
but put 'em in songs not file 'em on a fuckin' shelf!

***

47

2.

Derum Derum. Work will be a shock. He can mock my *fussy ways.*
My insistence in persisting to duplicate into the diary. Daily.

Manually. Not relying on a computer paid dividends. Power cut.
Two words but cruel. Metaphorically speaking. Melanie disagrees.

… She's been a good wife and mother although fails to appreciate
hierarchical structures: without, all would fall about our
                                                    proverbial ears.

Mind, her views were validated when I was pipped to the post
                                                    by a slip
of a girl to whom I taught Dewey's classified, correction, decimal

classification system, my years of service disregarded for a machine
whizz-kid! I am not technically retarded. I have learnt
                                        sufficient for my needs.

Computers will not help you tackle miscreants, the failed-fine
                                                    brigade,
the mark-a-page brigade, the turn-down-a-corner cohort. I can
                                        spot their sort:

not workers, shirkers. My son is fast becoming the latter no
                                        matter how I try
to persuade. He does not listen. I am afraid for his future. All
                                                    he desires

is to bang on blasted drums. *Derum, derum, derum-derum-derum.* I
                                                    suggested
the military with his 2:1 in history. Achieving even that
                                        miserable pass he needed

intensive coaching. Expensive. Not that he cares. He appears
                                                    unaware of all
except *derum,derum, derum-derum-derum.* His sister is a different
                                                    kettle of fish

yet I fail to understand why she became involved with that
                                        superannuated hippy
Zak who stud-plugs every orifice and ties a purple ribbon
                                        round his neck.

Of course I refused. I am fond of my daughter. Why would I
                                        desire to see her
shackled to a creature who can only pen poor verses
                                        on…bodily matters.

I try to correct him, having an honours, but he mocks parsing
                                        a poem. Calls it
…*selective arsing*. He laughs. My son does a drum roll. My
                                        daughter laughs too.

If I remonstrate she rounds on *me*, flounces from the room in
                                        a fashion
she has never done before. And all the time that incessant
                                        sound. *Derum.*

Melanie takes their part. He has won all their hearts. He smiles
                                        not smirks,
which he does when we're alone. He tells my son money is the
                                        root of all evil.

If I mention the brutal fact that songs do not buy bread they
                                        chant, *Yeah, yeah.*
Can't buy me love! and misquote scripture, *Man cannot live* etc.

Before he came I used to say we were the perfect picture of a
                                        loving family.
When young, I sang in a choir. Composed…. Taking the long view….

***

3.

Why do men of a certain age wear beige?
What's happened to the purple Zak and I gave
for his birthday pressie? Thought he'd appreciate irony.

When I grow old…? Nation's favourite? Obviously not his.
He's got to accept Zak. Accept the fact we're together.
Not only her hand, was trying for a man-to-man joke.

But he did buy a tie especially to ask you, father.
Pity it was purple. Now you think we're laughing at you.
Like my useless brother. He's not really. Having a laugh.

He carries that family photograph when he goes to gigs.
You know, our alpine yodelling one. You pretending
to ogle the bovines….He was so hurt when you….

His music thing. It's just a phase. He can't say
he needs praise so he feels compelled to rebel.
It's an act. One day, when he's a man, he'll confess

he knows drumming a pub isn't being a professional.
He'll settle. If he still goes on about being pro
make him pay his share. Say it's only fair.

That'll make him flick his hair! Can we go back
to Zac, father? I've read it's hard for a man to part
with his daughter but I would have left home some day

whether to be married… or not. You and mother need space.
Look at her poor face. It'll need more than cream
to bring her peace. My brother's not an angel

but you can be really anal, father…. I'll never
tell you all this and I hear my drummer-brother's
Derum-derum…Dad! *Your* face? It's…slipped! Dad? Dad?

***

50

4.

I have seen his bottom broaden
his trousers sag beneath the weight
his cheeks travel from tight butt to flop
his belt loosened yearly by a notch
his face become a steady-redder
blotch between ears that have heard
Not this time, John. Stiff competition.
but no word of reproach for that oaf
in the office. Service Manager, my foot!

He has come home numb with worry
but always read the children a story
listened to my daily tales of trivial acts
with rapt attention, his eyes glistened
when the hamster died, he carried a bird
with a broken wing five miles over hills
to a vet in the nearest town only to find
when he set it down it had died so he took
it back, returned it to the same woods…

Last night, in his study, I saw him claw
a book from the shelf, break its binding.

RECESSION

1.

A slow decline, not of love or living
but sensibility toward each and every.
This is lack: the way a frost smothers
 the garden, denies the crocus to blaze,
the snowdrop to show her cowled head:
the frost where a lover leaves unsaid
the one word or a child, clinging, looks
upwards, eyes entreating for a simple
sweet, finding indifference, weeps.

2.

Between these lines lie the times
we do not mention, those times
when we once lay, unblemished
in silk and stone-washed denim
crushing long grass where windfalls
now wait, bruised beneath skin,
for the pecking of sharp beaks.

DRIVING

This is not dappled light but a flaw
to scar eyes, blinding each
bend, leaving to chance

the unseen: a rickle of bones marks
the undulating highway, the way
the unsaid hangs in the air.

WARNING

Why did you think this house was forever?
Sun gives way to rain, pointing loosens,
walls crumble: outsiders may bring hope

of renewal but the price prohibits. So far all
seems merely cosmetic but the way paper
ripples on fresh plaster, a door frame hangs

or an opening sticks without reason, requires
immediate diagnosis: during dry periods root
damage may ensue especially if *terra firma*

is mainly clay: temporary measures will disguise
subsidence but aeration activates preservation.
Draw upon every current insurance policy
before smoke ghosts from disused chimneys.

!

ARTERY

The railway line flanks roads where houses, terraced,
substantial, guard each others' warmth, close doors
against unwonted draughts and hurried feet passing

beyond midnight. Yet wind creeps in unsuspecting places:
bends the branch to scratch a window that holds at bay
the further dark, holds within a dark beyond admittance.

ROUTE 493

The wet wait was long but no one spoke.
Diving ever-deeper into overcoats contact
remained elusive yet the distant sighting
rendered a collective sigh, echoed again
when the doors open to expose a scowl
of a man not disposed to allow inside
a sodden queue who propose to enter
despite his best endeavour.
                                    They slop on.
Each seeks the safety of his seat before
the driver releases the brake, shudders
all toward their hoped-for destination.

Sometimes it's the inarticulate incidental
which unleashes the unacknowledged
towards an imperceptible blet, mediates
between what is known, what suppressed:
acquiesces in desire made manifest.

So it is on the 493 where common meets
non-common: the first lurch urges the bus
onto the verge, is greeted with a grimace.
An apology diffuses any situation. Mistakes
happen no matter what a person's station
but a further slide tends toward accusation,
the driver said to smell of drink being taken.
Protestations of sobriety
                                    by the passengers
– never did a bus carry such piety – clears
his scowl: such wanton words determine
all toward their pre-ordained destination.

It could be said that aforesaid inarticulate
incidental is capable of showing sympathy
unless it's simply coincidental: an electric
circuit proving solidarity with a flat battery

to deny a flicker of light to all but the driver
who quivers a scissor-smile, reveals teeth,
black, but one, back, pearl-white, redeems
the void from where a Requiem, Mahler's,
hums the air. Upright Anthea, her education
classical, forged by Radio 3, recognises
implications in such a choice and prepares
herself to give voice as does Mr. Bhattacharjee
but those untutored
                    in the wider world of Kashmiri
saffron, knowing nothing of Kali's omniscience,
are unaware of the creative force that lies behind
destruction, await their fate.
                              Lizzie, fleet fugitive
from rent arrears, amazes with her profound
knowledge of language in a range not usually
found on route 493 when Mr. Bhattacharjee
trips, knocks from her firm grip the drip's
silver stand, her constant companion: her life.

Darkness droops over each shoulder: shawls
strangers: mutually neutral ground is invaded.
Consideration of others has always been a mark
of Mr. B. He who had treasured his case of silken
pleasures up the tiny terraced paths of unknown
'50's cities', the case – ripped on the Karachi
carousel that was *his* life – bound by string,
he who took care
                    to close every gate now finds
his fine-veined hand hits Anthea's feathered hat.
Apologetic Bhattacharjee entreats forgiveness,

reflects upon fate, deflects attention by scorning
graffiti adorning seats, voices common concern
Council should put firm foot down with heavy hand.
Anthea does not mock the urban aesthetic, verbal
or visual, appreciates her generation's philosophy
is sculpted by a hole in a rock designated *Woman.*

She reaches out to embrace each new conception felt
deep in her womb. At night, away from life's hectic traffic
she lays naked on static sheets, electric with anticipation
for the God of Creation to penetrate her inner being. Now
she sweeps ample arms wide, *We must never be afraid*
to be receptive to each other, to discover that connective
essence, sister to sister, brother to brother. Clasp hands!
Darkness is our friend.

                  The driver, ever-compliant with such
sentiment, fades the last of the light, faces the disarrayed:
Do not be dismayed. Your accusations, unfounded, pre-empt
you toward a pre-ordained destination. No one is exempt.

Archive

YOU WANT LIFE WRITING?

Fulham-born, you know from three not to hang
upside down on the rusty monkey bars displaying
your ha'penny peeping under saggy navy knickers
or stray too near the bushes where the war-lost waited.

Beyond the railway a dark mass played host to debris
jettisoned from passing cargo boats, cans serrated
an oil slick we called river but no fish called home,
its summer stench enhanced by the coal yard

where, swift as a river, we secreted small lumps.
Black slag covered our clothes earning a quick cuff,
slow kiss, for the precious hoard fished from pockets,
– lit only when we woke to ice crazing inside a window.

That first real winter's day, we coddled close, watched
legs mottle, removed a layer of cloth, scarf or hat,
a prop to wrap around a fist for Mr. Punch. Safe.
Summer play-out or graveyard autumn dark,

the park, the streets, all uncertain, yet the house
space was displaced by the unhoused, blitzed friends
who came late, lingered on the unlit stair and we awake,
aware of creaking board, the step that doesn't move away.

ON READING HACKER'S *CANCER WINTER*
IN THE BARENTS SEA

My left. Your right. Such malignancy we
harbour deep within erogenous zones:
independent existence, unpaired, un
-stable, highly reactive, complex style:
where's the natural habitat for free
radicals? Within a free radical
exiled lesbian feminist jew: France.

Essays on Departure, an avid read,
not so bad for this kid who never did
hang into daily school, desiring dark
interiors, Earls Court, Charing X, roads
that led beyond schoolbook literacy
to learn haphazard life styles from ladies
– not exiled lesbian feminist jews –

who plied nightly but between tricks could cut
a line or quote two from Ferlinghetti,
Gunn, blind Milton bemoaning loss of sight,
beloved of kind Sara whose humpback
brought bouquets; sisters gave coded caution,
Do not go gentle into that good night
allow only lovers kiss open lips,

either love/loathe, there is no in-between,
mode, median, mean, statistician speak,
is not an option: Sadie unbuttoned
wisdom, dispensed erudition, eased
unpalatable truths between fingers
rolling rizlas: friends forever, or not,
but for what I have received may the Lord....

...and I *am* truly thankful for you who
have never known these women but listen
while in darkness we tentatively grope
around one more icy town, donning spikes,
seeking certainties over uncertain
ground, old lovers cautiously cruising
fjords, thrusting further north, no wiser

than when we first began those betrayals,
denials, protestations: words rehearsed
covering uncovered parts, convicted.
Yet still we thrust, gentle, slippy fingers
into uncharted waters, depth soundings
reveal dissonance not smooth cadences
of exiled lesbian feminist jews:

France.

* Dylan Thomas

SUCCESSION

That night rain slicked tarmac, pounded
down stairs we pounded down, falling
to where we all fell, tail-flick eyes

noting undulating buttocks,
marking which butch protectorate,
slackened by drink, lay open: invasion,

colonial-smooth, involved drinks involved
vodka laced with rum downed in one
– last butch still standing was king.

Water replacing Smirnoff left
no doubt as regards the victor.
Frankie, dumb after the eighth shot,

stumbled on tenth, fell on the fourteenth:
Backs splayed against the bar,
we watched Ellery,

king Ellery, butch supremo, tip
bar staff strategically substituting
voddi-water-voddi every other order,

winking as Frankie gave solemn permission
for one dance with her babe.
The Babe.

Imperceptibly, Ellery
guided both of them just beyond
voddi-vision-blur before the deliberate grope

under Babe's skirt. The roar shattered optics.
Movers 'n shakers 'n myopics
saw Ellery eating floor

mouthing *Balls. Babe's got…*
The swayback of Frankie above
There ain't no gender in luv 'n there ain't no trust

where there's lust. Her flick came from nowhere.
That night blood slicked. Awe held us fast:
a pin dropped: Frankie reigned.

IN MEMORIAM

i.m. L. A. Wiggins and W. H. Wiggins

I remember:
        the hair fine, a loose bun,
spun-white floss such as no pier head
had produced, cheekbones high, skin
blushed, no artifice needed;

I remember:
        the chair, small-wheeled,
canvas taut over high-backed frame,
day-long trips easing onto early evening
pub or saunter in the park, the keeper
suspicious, eyeing your trailing hand
casually clutching the lavender bush
but unable to challenge a nonagenarian
with the face of an angel;

I remember:
        restrictions: your cataract operation,
protracted six week blackout, all light feared:
the surgeon (female) deified: Matron's word on the ward, God's.
Under 8? Wait here.

I remember:
        the commando-crawl under beds,
floor dust free, surfacing at yours, hauled, hidden beneath blanket.
In the middle of a Nightingale ward I slept.

I remember:
        singing *The Man who Broke the Bank at Monte Carlo*
long before I learnt *Three Little Piggies Went to Market.*

I remember:
        the sudden swoop of spit and scrub.

I remember:
            antihistamine undiscovered,
a G.P. too unconfident to perform a tracheostomy,
left death certain. Pressed against my grotesque tongue,
blocking airways, the wooden spatula snapped, replaced
with your one silver teaspoon, your very best; EPNS.
In the morning it told me something momentous had happened
– like having two, blue twists of saltin my crisps.

So certain was death,
the doctor's morning-round bag contained my signed certificate.
                                    He took forever to recover.

His next visit found you both, two peas in a pod, top to toe in bed,
double pneumonia: a 'dead' child kneeling beside, hands joined.

I remember:
            naming an egg 'albumen' shared between us three.

I remember
            skipping over rubble of war-torn houses
to where the 'runner' waited to take Grandad's tanner
– all hope pinned on teenage Piggott for the National.

I remember:
            lugging the acid battery across the main road
to be charged by Mister Drangonisi, who bowed, clicked his heels
on opening the door to this seven year old, gruffly warned,
                                    Be careful. Slop not.
Safely home we three sat close: *Saturday Night Theatre!*

I remember:
            being 'sent down', not chastised or advised but simply,
If we're able to place a morsel on the table there will be a space for you.

I do not remember love. I live with that.

MONTE

i.m. L. A. Wiggins

You wouldn't like it. Not now. No twenties glitz.
No mansions but flats so close you could talk
to your neighbour without leaving your bed.
It's Naples *sans* knickers on the line –
the perspective as different as Dali to Dupré.

FROM THE FRIDGE

Shrink wrapped. Just. But no discernible contours. It oo-oo-oo-zed.
A shape-shifter waiting escape. It did. It seeped. A slow-slick curling
lip of thin wrapper. No Attar of Roses. Granny would've
                                                    disapproved.

I recoiled faster than that snake hearing God in the Garden of
                                                    Eden,
faster than Adam's snatch of fig leaves and Eve lolling naked
                                                    as a kid
in 1889, on a midnight beach where Elizabeth London, being
                                                    named
by birthplace, swam out to grab a frightened child, while other
                                                    orphans
wandered in the negligent care of Bessie Toogood, unfurling
                                                    her hair
for a lover who knew a shrewd woman, one able to use the old ruse
eddgycatin' the childer in the glories of natcher. that so impressed
Mrs. Scrim, Superintendent, content with gin and an evening empty
of bloody kids – *if they don't all return, well, what's a name struck
through a line in a ledger or next poor beggar dumped at the door
inheriting it* – knowing as long as she keeps her gin well-hidden,
food bills down, any clown would be content to have her herd her
precious sheep toward a prize destiny, servant at the big house,
the same house where his Lordship, encountering a fail-to-curtsey
-aged-six-Lily, ordered she should walk sharp donkey-dung-cobbles
clogs slung around her neck – yet better than her own grandmother
fared being birched, strung under a horse's belly, driven
                                                    around town,
for taking a single cube of sugar from her own family's oak table.

Such a heritage! Lily being Grandmother who, by the way,
                                                    never wore
Attar of Roses, demands immediate action – so I threw out
                                                    the fridge.

TRANSGRESSION

After, he panned across the violet hills
watched rainclouds advancing stealthily
cows folding down in fields.

He knew the time to return was certain
as milking or lambs in spring. He knew
the innocence of spring

flying towards him, arms outstretched
demanding a high-flying-angel ride,
ice-cream lacing a bud-mouth.

RECIPROCATION

Absolution was sought in walking the mountain
– begun at the bamboo-straw hut, the chai

bitter. The woman flicked her eyes towards
the way ahead, stopped as an engine's whine

dwindled behind, remained out of sight. The glass
returned she inclined her body but did not meet

his eyes. The pass, saddleback, single-track,
denied him the privilege of other walkers but a bird

shadowed his steps, a companion in the light-shrink
of night, the mountain bruted from blue to purple,

the village many miles behind, the refuge just beyond
the only car to glide by, windows tinted, lights flashing.

CLOSURE

Enclosed in these hours, two p.m. until six,
she waits, patiently, for houses to greet
incoming earners, the street light to throw
its tolerant glow. She realises the necessity
to take a slop of tea before granting herself
permission – a first whisky to dismantle
the solitary: defining the day's cornerstone....